Fine Art Store 15 April 89

HANDBOOK OF PICTORIAL SYMBOLS

3,250 EXAMPLES FROM INTERNATIONAL SOURCES

RUDOLF MODLEY

With the assistance of

WILLIAM R. MYERS

Dover Publications, Inc., New York

NOTICE

The Olympic sports pictogram symbols appearing on pages 96 (bottom two rows and symbol on right, third row from bottom), 100 (bottom three rows and fourth row from bottom except symbol on left), and 101 (top three rows) are marks and worldwide copyrights of the Canadian Olympic Association. The symbols may only be used by permission and/or license from the Canadian Olympic Association. Permission and/or licenses may be obtained through their financial affiliate: Olympic Trust of Canada, 2 St. Clair Avenue West, Toronto, Ontario M4V 1L5, Telephone 416-967-6681.

The five Olympic rings on page 96 (fourth row from the top, second symbol from the right) and any designs incorporating these five Olympic rings (e.g. pages 123 and 124) may only be used by permission and/or license from the National Olympic Committee of the country in which they are to be used.

Published in the United Kingdom by Constable and Company, Ltd., 10 Road, Don Mills, Toronto, Ontario.
Published in the United Kingdom by Constable and Company, Ltd., 10 Orange Street, London WC 2.
Handbook of Pictorial Symbols; 3,250 Examples from International Sources is a new work, first published by Dover Publications, Inc., in 1976.

DOVER *Pictorial Archive* SERIES

This book belongs to the Dover Pictorial Archive Series. You may use the designs and illustrations for graphics and crafts applications, EXCLUDING THE PICTO'GRAFICS SYMBOLS APPEARING ON PAGES 101–09 (ALSO SCATTERED THROUGHOUT SECTION III, MARKED BY THE ABBREVIATION "Pg") AND THE OLYMPIC SPORTS PICTOGRAM SYMBOLS MENTIONED IN THE NOTICE ON THIS PAGE, free and without special permission, provided that you include no more than ten in the same publication or project. (For permission for additional use, please write to Dover Publications, Inc., 31 East 2nd Street, Mineola, N.Y. 11501.)

However, republication or reproduction of any illustration by any other graphic service whether it be in a book or in any other design resource is strictly prohibited.

Picto'grafics are copyright © 1974 by Paul Arthur, VisuCom Ltd. For permission to use any of these symbols, address Paul Arthur, VisuCom Ltd., Toronto M3C 2K5.

International Standard Book Number: 0-486-23357-X
Library of Congress Catalog Card Number: 76-15438

Manufactured in the United States of America
Dover Publications, Inc.
31 East 2nd Street
Mineola, N.Y. 11501

INTRODUCTION
TO GRAPHIC SYMBOLS

There are several different kinds of graphic symbols. Many are simple, dramatic, illustrative. Quite often they are pictorial or "iconic," simplified reproductions of objects or concepts (see Figure 1). But graphic symbols do not necessarily have to be pictorial. Some very effective ones can be called "image-related." While somewhat abstract, they retain a certain visual relationship with the object or act which they represent; for instance, double wavy horizontal lines standing

Figure 1. Graphic symbols can be simple and dramatic. (De Delver, Beeldstatistick, *1935, No. 2. Designed by Gerd Arntz.)*

for "water." Finally, there are "abstract" or "arbitrary" symbols, which have no visual relationship to the objects or concepts they represent. To this category belong most of our letters and numerals, the punctuation marks, and mathematical operators, such as the plus and minus signs.

Graphic symbols can do many things for us. Quantitative data can be expressed through the repetition of graphic symbols. Groups of symbols can be arranged to show, for example, simple historical series, somewhat more complicated statistical breakdowns, or the geographical distribution of data (see Figures 2, 3 and 4).

Graphic symbols can also be utilized to show processes. Figures 5 and 6 demonstrate that the pictorial content of such presentations can be minimal—or even completely absent.

The modern techniques of graphic presentation of facts and figures were developed by Otto Neurath in the early 1920's in Vienna. If you learn these techniques, you too can use graphic symbols to set forth complex facts in simplified, more easily understood and more easily remembered form.

In addition to the symbols which can help you *tell your story,* there are others which *talk to you.* Just think what happens when you read these lines. The letters of our alphabet, formed into meaningful words, talk to you. The letters of the alphabet (and the numerals) are so much a part of our daily life that we hardly think of them as graphic symbols. But, of course, they are just that. We do not show them in this volume because they

1911-14
1915-18
1919-22
1923-32

Figure 2. By showing quantities of symbols, statistical facts can be expressed clearly and simply: This chart, in which each symbol represents 2500 marriages, shows the average annual number of marriages in Vienna from 1911 through 1932. (Gesellschafts- und Wirtschaftsmuseum, Vienna. Designed by Gerd Arntz, about 1933.)

are fully accepted and well known to the literate world. But we go into considerable detail about new systems of graphic symbols which are now being developed; some day, we hope, many of these new "public symbols" will be well known to literates and illiterates alike (Figure 7). You have already encountered some of them in your daily life—on highways, at airports, in hospitals, factories, schools and, more and more often, on pack-

ages, clothing, appliances, and so forth.

In the largely illiterate pre-modern world, pictorial symbols were the main visual guides for strangers who came into town and needed to find the shops of the baker, the barber, the apothecary—or even the pawnbroker. Today, in spite of increased literacy, many thousands of travelers are, in fact, illiterate in countries whose language they do not know and whose alphabet they may not even be

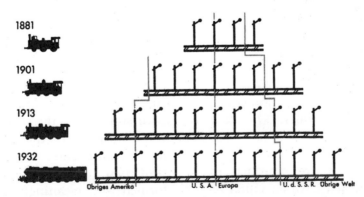

1881
1901
1913
1932

Figure 3. Statistical symbols can be used in combination with "explanatory" graphic symbols. This chart expresses the amount of railroad trackage throughout the world in 1881, 1901, 1913 and 1932. The distance between each "signal" symbol stands for 100,000 kilometers of track. (Gesellschafts- und Wirtschaftsmuseum, Vienna.)

able to decipher. There is, therefore, a need for graphic symbols to lead us to the nearest telephone, to help us claim our baggage or find an elevator.

The number of these public symbols is increasing rapidly. Some are accepted widely, some are not. There are even different symbols representing the same thing, and identical symbols standing for different concepts. Efforts are now underway to standardize the most important symbols into a "new universal language" through international efforts of careful selection, design, testing and education.

THE CONTENT AND ARRANGEMENT OF THIS BOOK

Part One of this volume deals with pictorial symbols, showing over 1300 examples. Part Two (pages 53-137) contains an extensive survey of public symbols.

In Part One you will find symbols representing almost every facet of human existence, from having a baby to committing suicide, and from growing the most nourishing vegetable to perpetrating the most heinous crime. These pictorial symbols have been drawn from two sources. The bulk of them (those on pages 3-45) come from a publication of the Pictograph Corporation of New York, entitled *1000 Pictorial Symbols* (1942, second enlarged edition, 1943). These symbols were designed in the 1930's and early 1940's under the direction of Rudolf Modley by Karl Koehler, Henry Adams Grant, John Carnes and others. In this volume we have followed the arrangement by subject category used in *1000 Pictorial Symbols*. The second source (pages 46-52) is a publication of The Netherlands Foundation for Statistics, entitled *Graphische Voorstellingen* (Graphic Symbols), The Hague, not dated. They constitute a representative selection of the symbols used by the Vienna Social and Economic Museum and its Netherlands successor institutions. Practically all of these symbols were designed under the direction of Otto Neurath by Gerd Arntz. These symbols are randomly arranged, but they are fully indexed.

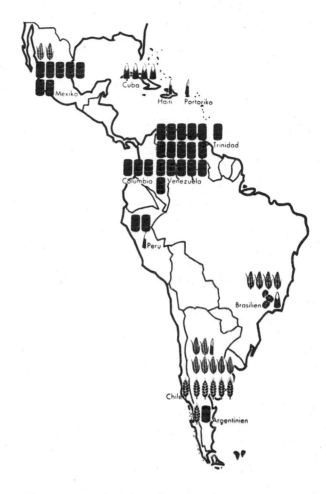

Figure 4. Symbols can be placed on maps to relate quantitative data to appropriate geographical areas. This illustration was prepared to indicate quantities of oil, sugar, grain, corn and coffee exported from various Latin American countries. (De Delver, Beeldstatistick, *1935, No. 2. From an article by Otto Neurath on Isotype.)*

The selection of public symbols in this book (Part Two) comes largely from a 1974 study called *Symbol Signs* prepared by the American Institute of Graphic Arts for the United States Department of Transportation. The first part of this study (reproduced in our Section III, pages 55-74) arranges the symbols according to service or facility: that is, it groups together all the various symbols for telephone, restroom, coffee shop and 32 other basic facilities culled from 25 different symbol systems in use at airports, railroad stations, world's fairs, Olympic games, and so forth.

The second part of the Department of

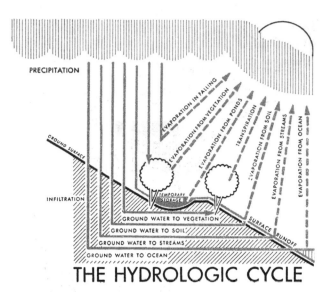

THE HYDROLOGIC CYCLE

Figure 5. Graphic symbols can also be used to show processes and flows. (From H. S. Person's Little Waters, *U. S. Soil Conservation Service. Government Printing Office, Washington, D.C., 1935-36. Graphics and design by Rudolf Modley and Henry Adams Grant.)*

Transportation study (our Section IV, pages 75-127) displays each of these 25 symbol systems individually. We have been able to supplement this section substantially from additional sources, so that many more than the 35 basic symbols are shown for some of the systems.

Section V of this volume (pages 128-137) contains symbols from four important graphic systems not included in the 1974 Department of Transportation study, plus symbols from two other frequently encountered systems: the Department of Transportation Hazard Labels and the United States Weather Bureau cloud code charts.

Excluded from consideration in this volume are thousands of graphic symbols developed by and designed for specialized and professional groups. Among these are the symbols used by architects, chemists, botanists and other scientific and professional workers. Among them, too, are the symbols of the astrologers and alchemists, the marks used on silver, china and paper, cattle brands, hobo symbols, and so forth. It is common to all these symbols that the circle of their users is limited and that they are, as a rule, arbitrary in their design—that is, that they are often without visual relationship to the objects or concepts which they represent.

Under the leadership of national standards organizations and the International Organization for Standardization in Geneva (ISO), specialized graphic "languages" have been developed for people working in the fields of electrical and electronic engineering, machine tools, plumbing, welding and dozens of other technical fields. The technical organizations themselves publish handbooks of their symbols, and many are also included in *Shepherd's Glossary of Graphic Signs and Symbols* (Dover, 1971). Shepherd excluded from his book the pictographic symbols with which this book is primarily concerned. On the other hand, Henry Dreyfuss, in his *Symbol Sourcebook* (McGraw-Hill, 1972) includes both pictorial and "professional" symbols.

Also outside the scope of this volume are experimental graphic languages, the two best known of which are Blissymbolics (C. K. Bliss, *Semantography,* Sydney, 1965) and LoCos (Yukio Ota, "LoCos," *Graphic Design,* Tokyo, June, 1971), although Jansen's Picto (1958) preceded them. A further, final

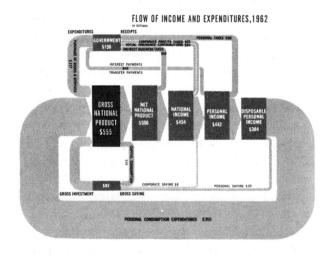

Figure 6. The diagrammatic flow techniques can be applied to simplify complex economic processes. (From U. S. A. and Its Economic Future *by Arnold B. Barach. A Twentieth-Century Fund Survey. Macmillan, New York, 1964. Graphics by Rudolf Modley, design by Stephen Kraft.)*

Figure 7. Four symbols that may become part of a new, international picture language, more widely understood and accepted than any alphabet. In this illustration, the gray represents red areas in the actual signs. (From Symbol Signs, prepared by the American Institute of Graphic Arts for the U. S. Department of Transportation, 1974, under the direction of William R. Myers. Designed by Cook and Shanosky.)

exclusion is the subject of trademarks, for although they are sometimes based on pictorial symbols, trademarks are private rather than public in their design and application and, moreover, are generally not pictorially usable.

BRIEF HISTORY OF GRAPHIC SYMBOLS

The public symbols in use today have had many forerunners. Examples would be the symbols used along ancient roadways and the rather numerous early railroad traffic-control devices. Of course, the development of the automobile gave rise to many new symbols. One of the first modern-day road sign systems was that devised by the Italian Touring Club in 1895. By 1900 a Congress of the International League of Touring Organizations in Paris was considering proposals for standardization of road signage. In 1909 nine European governments agreed on the use of the four pictorial symbols shown in Figure 8 to indicate "bump," "curve," "intersection," and "grade-level railroad crossing." The intensive work on international road signs that took place between 1926 and 1949 eventually led to the development of the European Road Signs included in this volume (pages 131-134). The United States developed its own road signage system, which was also adopted by several other nations. Recently, however, the United States has begun to introduce the standard pictographic international symbols in general use in Europe.

The two men who have done most for the rebirth of interest in the development of attractive and effective symbols and their logical applications are Otto Neurath, an Austrian, and Katzumie Masaru, a Japanese. Although both pictographs and public symbols have been used since early times, we may well call Otto Neurath the Father of Pictography and Katzumie Masaru the major force behind the development of international pictorial and public symbology.

Neurath developed graphic symbols because of his interest in education and economics. The highlights of his career were the creation of the Social and Economic Museum in Vienna (1924), the publication of *Gesellschaft und Wirtschaft* (Leipzig, 1930) and the creation of the ISOTYPE system. We have already seen some of his work in Figures 1-4. Katzumie, as art director of the Tokyo Olympics, released for use in future Olympic Games the symbols his staff of 30 young designers created in 1960. He has also been an influential advocate of symbols in articles in *Graphic Design* magazine.

Figure 8. The earliest international road danger signs, adopted in 1909. They indicate "bump," "curve," "intersection" and "grade level railroad crossing."

ON DEVELOPING NEW PICTOGRAPHS AND PUBLIC SYMBOLS

To would-be pictographers, we repeat the advice we gave readers of the first edition of *1000 Pictorial Symbols* in 1942. Do not think that a set of these symbols and a mass of facts is all you need to make an effective pictograph. It is not. You will have to:

   —analyze your facts, pick out the essential ones, drop those which are not needed.

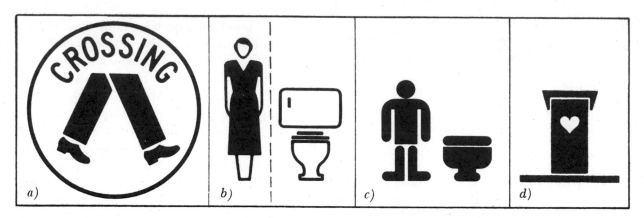

Figure 9. Pictorial symbols which might replace those traditionally used: a) Pedestrian Crossing (Australian Standard AS 1743-1975); b) Flush Toilet for Women, by Rudolf Modley; c) Flush Toilet for Men, by Gerhard Doerrié; d) Non-flush Toilet (Swedish Standard SIS 6131).

—select the one or more symbols that best pictorialize the facts. Avoid symbols that give no—or, worse yet, a false—impression about the object or fact you are trying to characterize.

—develop a layout which gets across the essential points of your story simply and quickly.

The Bibliography in this volume will be of value to all who are interested in studying this challenging field.

Persons who want to make up new public symbols should be aware that the creation of universally acceptable public symbols is an overwhelmingly difficult task. It requires organization, research, development, testing and evaluation, education and application. The inherent difficulties are dramatized by pointing out that many of the symbols included herein are only partially successful. Though widely used, many are still tentative; some have been adopted without benefit of one or more of the research and development steps which we consider essential.

One reason for badly conceived and ineffective public symbols is that administrators like to select symbols that have been used previ-ously by others, and which thus have presumably already been accepted by the public. This has led to the widespread adoption of some illogical or ambiguous symbols, such as the one showing a man and child to indicate "pedestrian crossing" and the use of a pictograph of a man to indicate "men's room" and of a woman to indicate "ladies' room." The "walking legs" Australian standard would appear to be a more logical choice for "pedestrian crossing"; after all, many different combinations of people are crossing roads and streets—and they all have legs to do so. As for toilets, it might help to have different symbols to indicate the specific type of facility—combined, where appropriate, with the symbol for man or woman (Figure 9).

At present a subcommittee of the International Standards Organization is at work on public symbols, and the literature on the subject is growing. It is hoped that the symbols collected in this volume will help pictographers as well as those at work on public symbols in their tasks.

Rudolf Modley
*Co-chairman, Glyphs, Inc.**

*Glyphs, Inc., RR1, Box 161, Kent, Ct. 06757, is a nonprofit organization for the development of universal graphic symbols. It does not design symbols but acts merely in an advisory capacity to others interested in the same objectives. It publishes a quarterly newsletter which is available free upon request. Margaret Mead and Rudolf Modley are co-chairmen of the organization.

BIBLIOGRAPHY

Aéroport de Paris, *Recueil de Pictogrammes Existants Correspondant a la Liste d'Informations de Base*. September, 1966.

Bertin, Jacques, *Semiologie Graphique.* Mouton et Gauthier-Villars, Paris, 1967.

Dreyfuss, Henry, *Symbol Sourcebook.* McGraw-Hill, New York, 1972.

Glyphs, Inc., *Newsletter* (a quarterly, since 1971). Kent, Connecticut 06757.

Hogben, Lancelot, *From Cave Painting to Comic Strip.* Chanticleer Press, New York, 1949.

Icographic. A quarterly review published by ICOGRADA (International Council of Graphic Design Associations). The Council also has a Commission on International Signs and Symbols. Address is 7 Templeton Court, Radnor Walk, Shirley, Croydon CR07 N2, England.

ISO (International Organization for Standardization), Technical Committee 145, Subcommittee 1, *Public Symbols.* The Secretariat for this Subcommittee is the Austrian Standards Institute, Postfach 130, A-1021 Wien, Austria.

Kepes, Gyorgy (ed.), *Sign, Image, Symbol.* Braziller, New York, 1966.

Koberstein, Herbert, *Wiener Methode der Bildstatistik, etc.* Bremen, 1969.

———, *Statistik in Bildern* (Statistics in Pictures). Poesche, Stuttgart, 1973.

Krampen, Martin, "Signs and Symbols in Graphic Communication." *Design Quarterly,* Walker Art Center, Minneapolis, 1965.

Mead, Margaret, and Modley, Rudolf, "Communication among all People Everywhere." *Natural History,* August-September, 1968.

Modley, Rudolf, *How to Use Pictorial Statistics.* Harper & Brothers, New York, 1937.

———, "World Language without Words." *Journal of Communication,* Autumn, 1974.

Modley, Rudolf, and Lowenstein, Dyno, *Pictographs and Graphs.* Harper & Brothers, New York, 1952.

Neurath, Otto, *International Picture Language.* Basic English Publishing Company, London, no date (about 1937).

———, *Basic by Isotype.* Basic English Publishing Company, London, 1948.

Shepherd, Walter, *Shepherd's Glossary of Graphic Signs and Symbols.* Dover Publications, Inc., New York, 1971.

U. S. Department of Transportation, *Symbol Signs.* National Technical Information Service, Springfield, Virginia, 1974.

Whitney, Elwood (ed.), *Symbology.* Hastings House, New York, 1960.

CONTENTS

Part One:
PICTORIAL SYMBOLS

Children, Youths

Children, Youths,
Boy Scouts, Sports

Teachers, Students, Education

Family Groups

    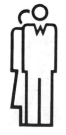

Immigrants and National Historical Types

Races, Nationalities, Religions

Blacks

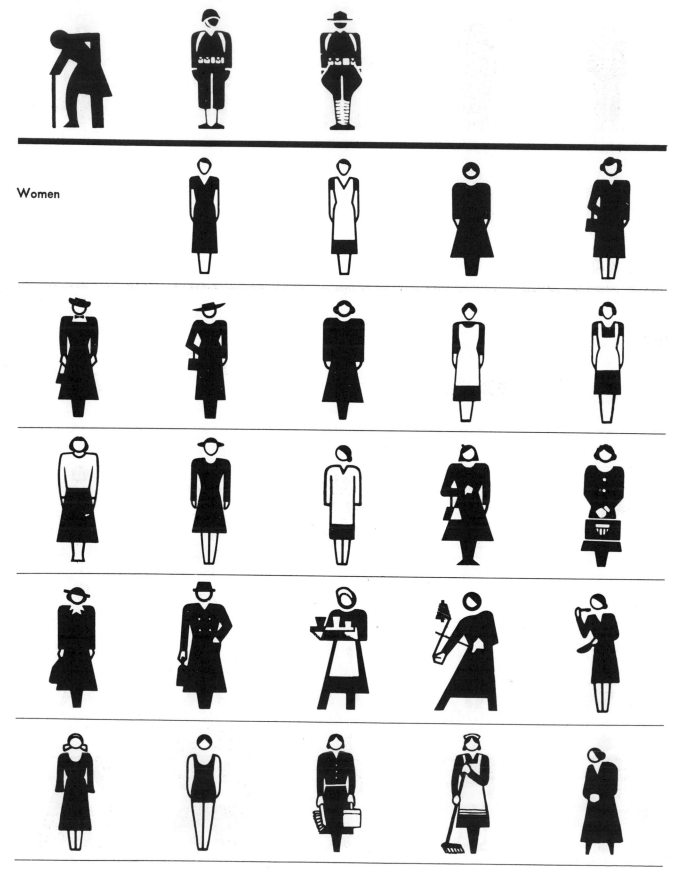

Women

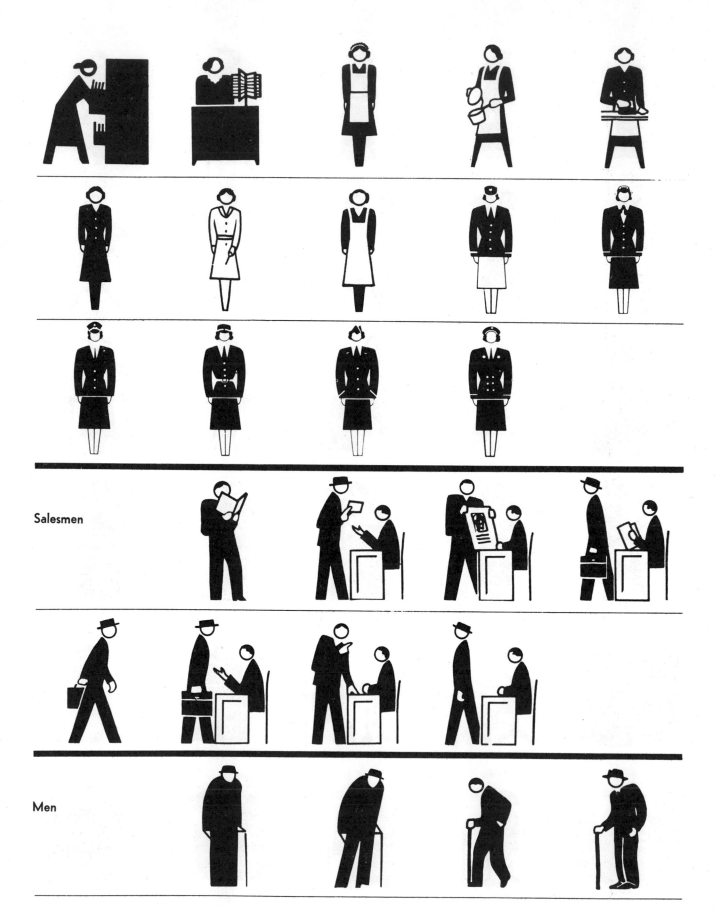

Salesmen

Men

Soldiers, Sailors, Aviators

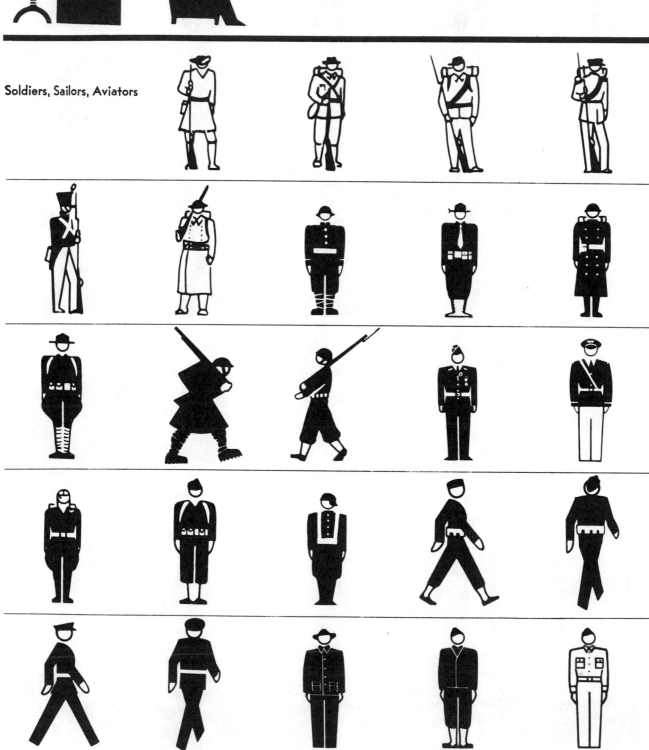

Military Equipment,
Insignia

Airplanes

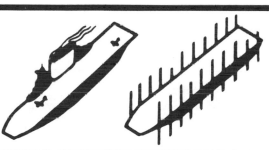

Naval Vessels

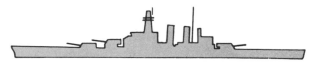

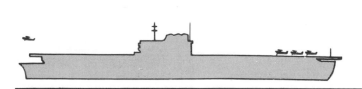

Merchant Vessels

Railroad Trains and Tracks

Autos and Other
Vehicles

Accidents

Sickness, Suicide, Death

Health

Meetings,
Conferences

Labor, Strikes

Farmers

Farm Machinery,
Land Use

 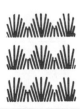   

Farm Products, Food,
Beverages, Tobacco

   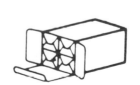 

Crime

Time, Jewelry and Miscellaneous Symbols

Money, Finance

Government and Politics

Government Buildings, Banks, Schools

Buildings (General),
Houses of Worship,
Houses, Stores

 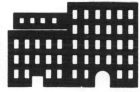  

   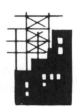 

  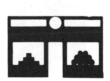  

Clothing, Toilet Articles

  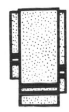  

Household Equipment,
Tools, Containers

    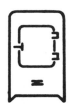

Machinery, Materials,
Products, Factories

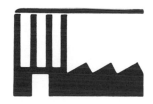

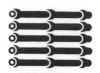   

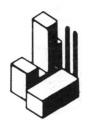    

**Entertainment,
Communication,
Recreation**

Animals, Insects

**Symbols by G. Arntz for
Netherlands Statistical
Foundation**

Car (historical)
Trowel (construction)
Sheep
Broom (housework)

Meat
Package
Jewelry
Leather

Pig
Brush
Milk
Cloth

Ink
Locomotive
Paper
Car

Ship
Medicine
Yarn
Airplane

Pottery
Electricity
Drink
Food basket

Bale
Compass
Extruded metal
Restaurant

Furniture
Crate
Hammer
House

Tire
Boat
Glass
Wheat

Undershirt
Shoe
Sugar cane
Lumber

Machine
Flour bag
Metal drum
Light

Range
Shuttle
Anvil
Cotton

Saw
Motor
Pot
Machine tool

Bridge
Glass
Radio
Coffee bean

Cup
Microscope
Skull
Shoe

Sign post
Village
Eye beam
Tin can

Milk can
Coil
Sheet
Plug

Jacket
Tailoring
Sugar loaf (historical)
Retort (chemicals)

Pot Ladle (foundry) Flower Lamp			
Chicken Tram TV Tin			
Tree Paint can Lemon Iron (for pressing)			
Horse Frame Flower Bucket			
Bar (metal) Bowl Airplane (historical) Book			
Gear Truck Jewelry Fish			

Factory
Winged wheel
  (transportation)
Leaf
Strawberry

Plow
Wine
Potato
Dredge

Ingots
Truck
Tractor
Bricks

Sickle
Sock
Light bulb
Stack

Scale
Cattle
Purse
Government (Dutch)

Meat
Tin can
Bicycle
Bread

Fruit	Barrel	Desk	Stove

Fruit
Barrel
Desk
Stove

   (stove)

Coil
Peas
Book
Bottle

Roll
Plumb line
Wall
Tape

Stack (coins)
Crown
Sailboat
Rice

Airplane
Cow
Glass
House

Cigarette
Washing machine
Mining
Factory

Tree
Cannon
Textile
Saw

Beet
Warehouse
Phone
Crane

Motorcycle
Wheel
Spool (wool)
Bed

Spool (cotton)
Knot
Burner
Sugar beet

Anchor
Jug
Elephant
Helicopter

Tree
Pretzel
Grinder

Part Two:
PUBLIC SYMBOLS

PUBLIC SYMBOL SYSTEMS
With their Designers or Consultants

[Many of these systems are the products of design staffs. Individual credit is given only when appropriate.]

ADCA, Australian Department of Civil Aviation. Kinneir, Calvert, and Associates.

ADV, German Airport Authority. M. Krampen and H. W. Kapitzki.

ATA, Air Transport Association. Arnold Thompson Associates.

BAA, British Airports Authority. Kinneir, Calvert, and Tuhill.

D/FW, Dallas-Fort Worth. Henry Dreyfuss Associates.

DOT'74, Department of Transportation, 1974. The American Institute of Graphic Arts, Cook and Shanoski Associates.

IATA, International Air Transport Association. Design staff.

ICAO, International Civil Aviation Organization. Design staff.

KFAI Sweden. Claes Tottie.

LVA, Las Vegas Airport. Richard Graef and John Follis.

NPS, National Park Service. Chermayeff and Geismar Associates.

NRR, Netherlands Railroad. Design staff.

O'64, Tokyo Olympic Games, 1964. Masaru Katzumie, Design Director; Yoshiro Yamashita, Designer.

O'68, Mexico Olympic Games, 1968. Manuel Villazón and Matthias Goeritz, Design Directors; Lance Wyman, Eduardo Terrazas and Beatrice Cole, Designers.

O'72, Munich Olympic Games, 1972. Otl Aicher, Design Director; Gerhard Joksch, Rolf Müller and Elena Winschermann, Designers.

Pg, Picto'grafics. Paul Arthur and Associates.

Port, Port Authority of New York and New Jersey. Design staff of the Aviation Department; Owen Scott, Graphic Designer.

SP, Swedish Standard Recreation Symbols. Kelvin Ekeland, Marie-Louise Halminen, Sven Lundström.

S/TA, Seattle-Tacoma Airport. Donald J. Gerands and Richardson Associates.

TA, Tokyo Airport. Aisaku Murakoshi.

TC, Transport Canada, Airports. Design staff of the Ministry of Air Transportation.

UIC, International Union of Railways. Design staff.

WO'72, Sapporo Winter Olympics, 1972. Masaru Katzumie, Design Director; Yoshiro Yamashita and Fukuda Shigeo, Designers.

X'67, Montreal Expo 67. Paul Arthur and Associates.

X'70, Osaka Expo 70. Eknan Kenji, GK Industrial Design Institute, Isozaki Arata, Fukuda Shigeo.

Grenoble Winter Olympics, 1968. Roger Excoffon.

Nova Scotia Department of Tourism. Corporation ARC (International).

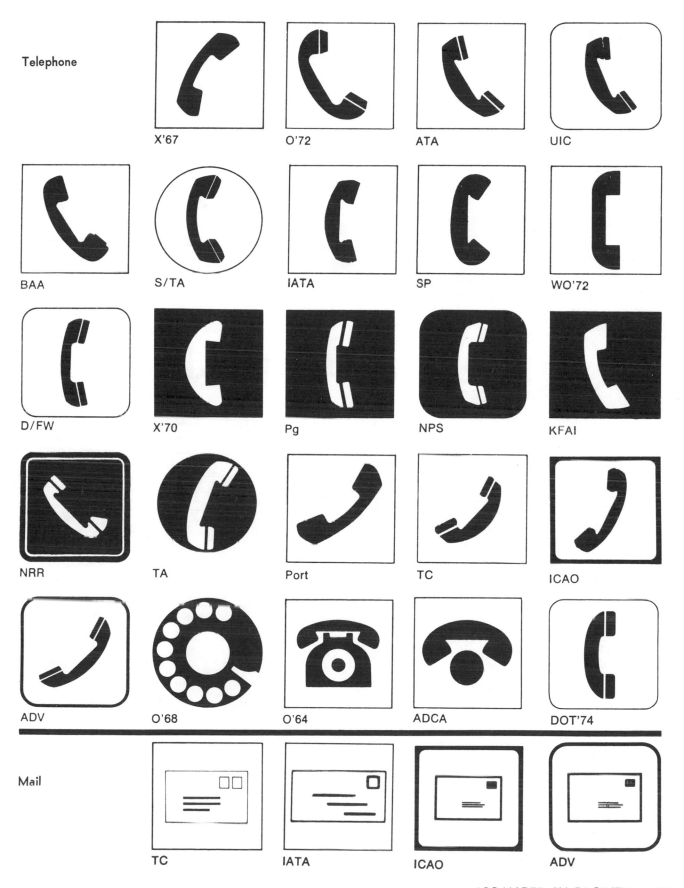

Telephone

X'67   O'72   ATA   UIC

BAA   S/TA   IATA   SP   WO'72

D/FW   X'70   Pg   NPS   KFAI

NRR   TA   Port   TC   ICAO

ADV   O'68   O'64   ADCA   DOT'74

Mail

TC   IATA   ICAO   ADV

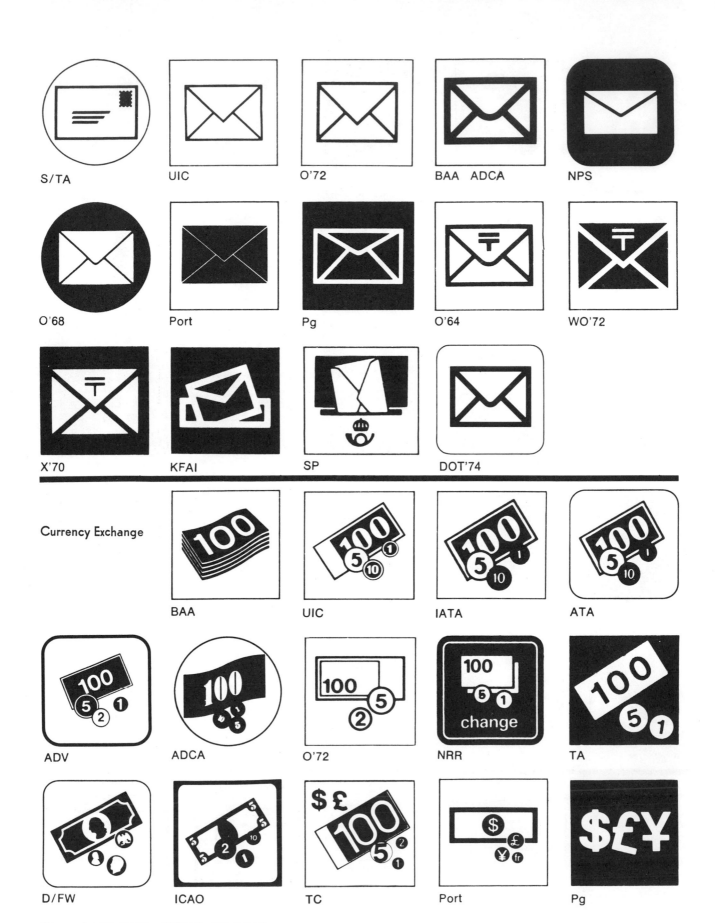

S/TA

UIC

O'72

BAA ADCA

NPS

O'68

Port

Pg

O'64

WO'72

X'70

KFAI

SP

DOT'74

Currency Exchange

BAA

UIC

IATA

ATA

ADV

ADCA

O'72

NRR

TA

D/FW

ICAO

TC

Port

Pg

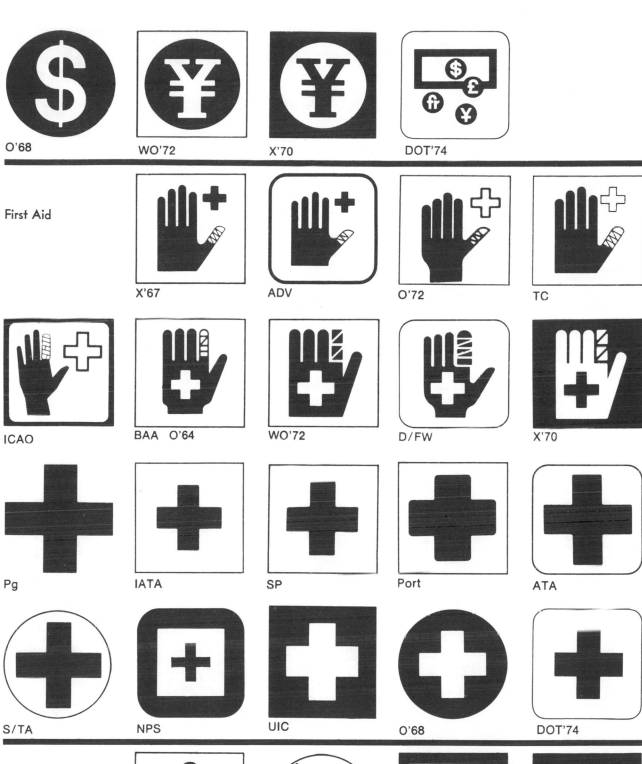

O'68

WO'72

X'70

DOT'74

First Aid

X'67

ADV

O'72

TC

ICAO

BAA O'64

WO'72

D/FW

X'70

Pg

IATA

SP

Port

ATA

S/TA

NPS

UIC

O'68

DOT'74

Lost and Found

X'67

S/TA

Pg

X'70

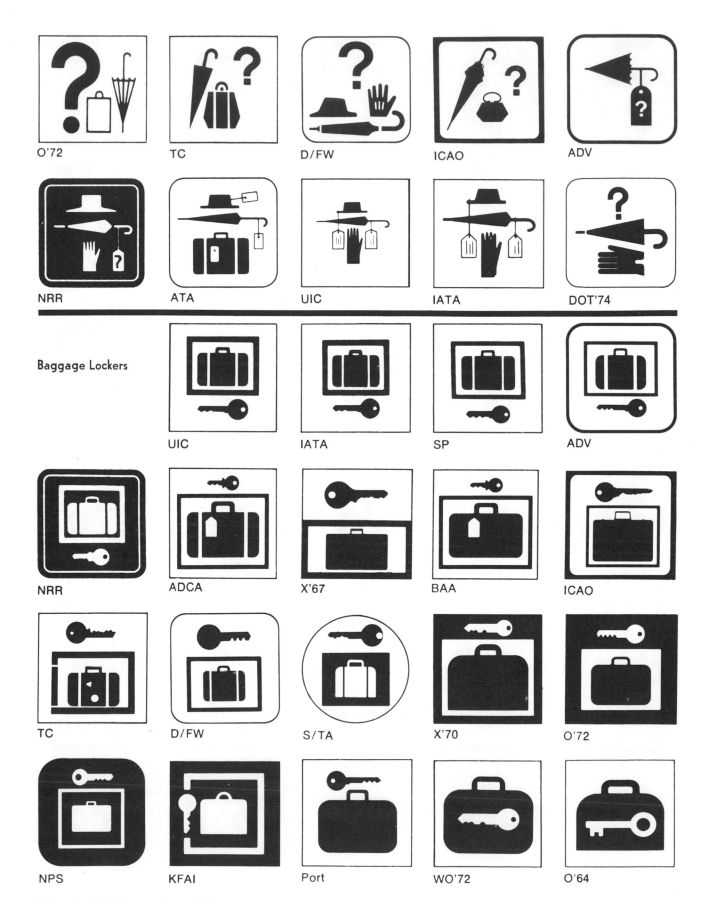

O'72

TC

D/FW

ICAO

ADV

NRR

ATA

UIC

IATA

DOT'74

Baggage Lockers

UIC

IATA

SP

ADV

NRR

ADCA

X'67

BAA

ICAO

TC

D/FW

S/TA

X'70

O'72

NPS

KFAI

Port

WO'72

O'64

Pg

DOT'74

Elevator

S/TA

D/FW

ATA

Pg

KFAI

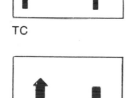
TC

ICAO

ADV

O'72

BAA

IATA

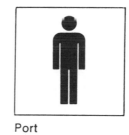
ADCA

DOT'74

Toilets, Men

WO'72

SP

Port

ICAO

O'72

ADV

O'64

KFAI

X'70

NPS   O'68   TA   BAA   UIC

IATA   ATA   D/FW   ADCA   S/TA

NRR   Pg   X'67   DOT'74

Toilets, Women   WO'72   Port   ICAO   X'70

O'68   BAA   ADCA   O'64   SP

O'72   TA   UIC   IATA   ATA

D/FW

ADV

S/TA

NPS

NRR

KFAI

Pg

X'67

DOT'74

Toilets

BAA

UIC

SP

KFAI

NRR

D/FW

TC

ICAO

O'64

ADV

Port

TA

DOT'74

Information

Port

O'68

D/FW

ATA

IATA

Pg

NPS

BAA   ADCA

S/TA

TA

X'70

O'72

KFAI

NRR

TC

UIC

SP

ADV

ICAO

WO'72

O'64

DOT'74

Hotel Information

ICAO

TC

D/FW

IATA

O'72

NPS

Pg

SP

DOT'74

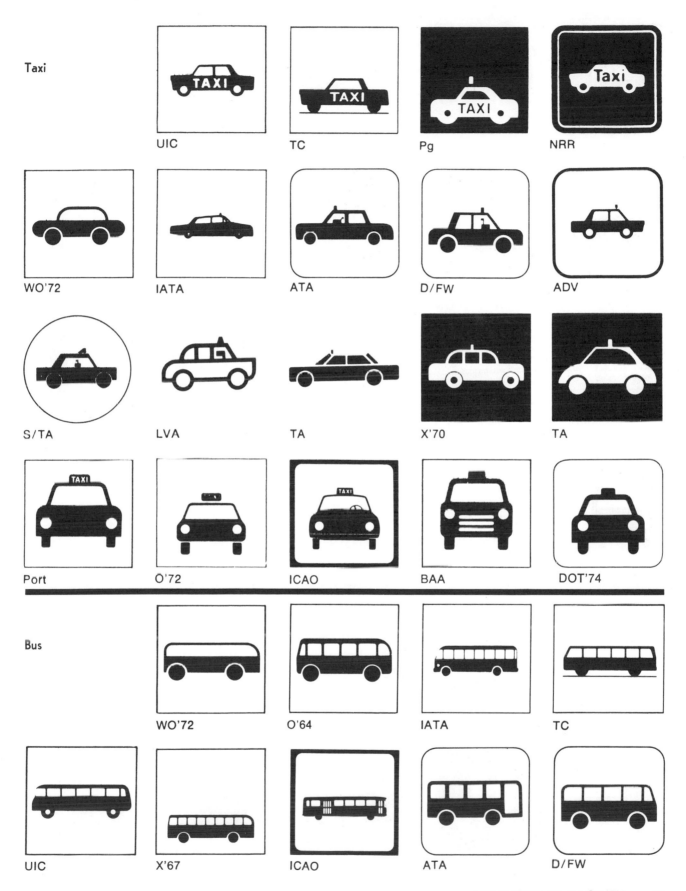

Taxi

UIC

TC

Pg

NRR

WO'72

IATA

ATA

D/FW

ADV

S/TA

LVA

TA

X'70

TA

Port

O'72

ICAO

BAA

DOT'74

Bus

WO'72

O'64

IATA

TC

UIC

X'67

ICAO

ATA

D/FW

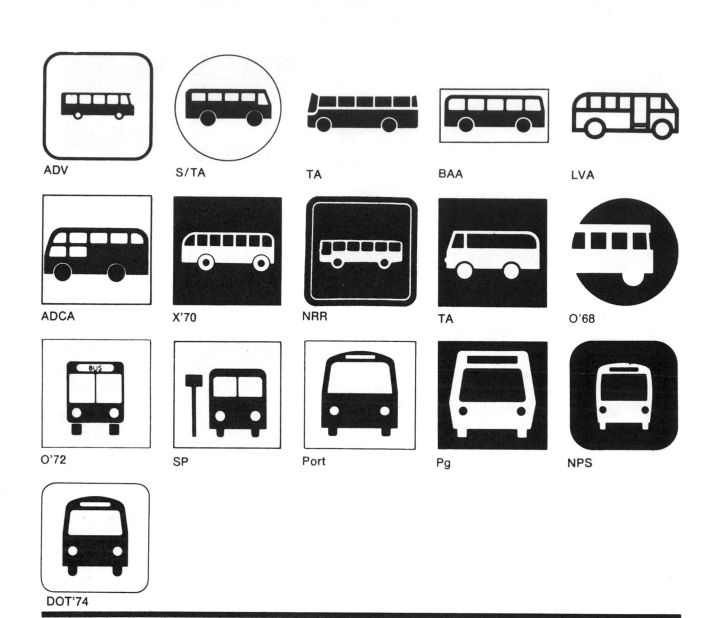

ADV

S/TA

TA

BAA

LVA

ADCA

X'70

NRR

TA

O'68

O'72

SP

Port

Pg

NPS

DOT'74

Ground Transportation

D/FW

DOT'74

Rail Transportation

Pg

SP

O'72

O'72

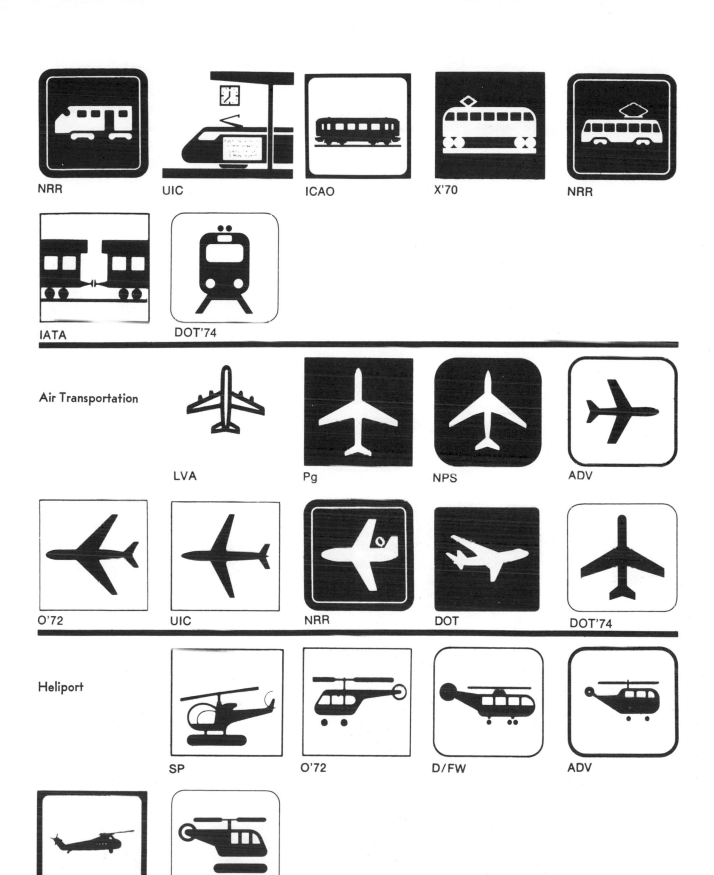

NRR

UIC

ICAO

X'70

NRR

IATA

DOT'74

Air Transportation

LVA

Pg

NPS

ADV

O'72

UIC

NRR

DOT

DOT'74

Heliport

SP

O'72

D/FW

ADV

ICAO

DOT'74

Water Transportation

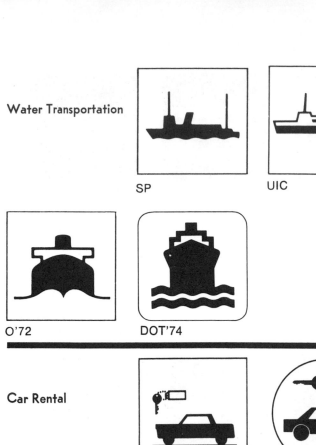

SP UIC X'67 Pg

O'72 DOT'74

Car Rental

TC S/TA D/FW ADV

ATA Pg TA BAA ADCA Port

O'72 ICAO NRR UIC DOT'74

rent a car

Restaurant

SP IATA UIC ICAO

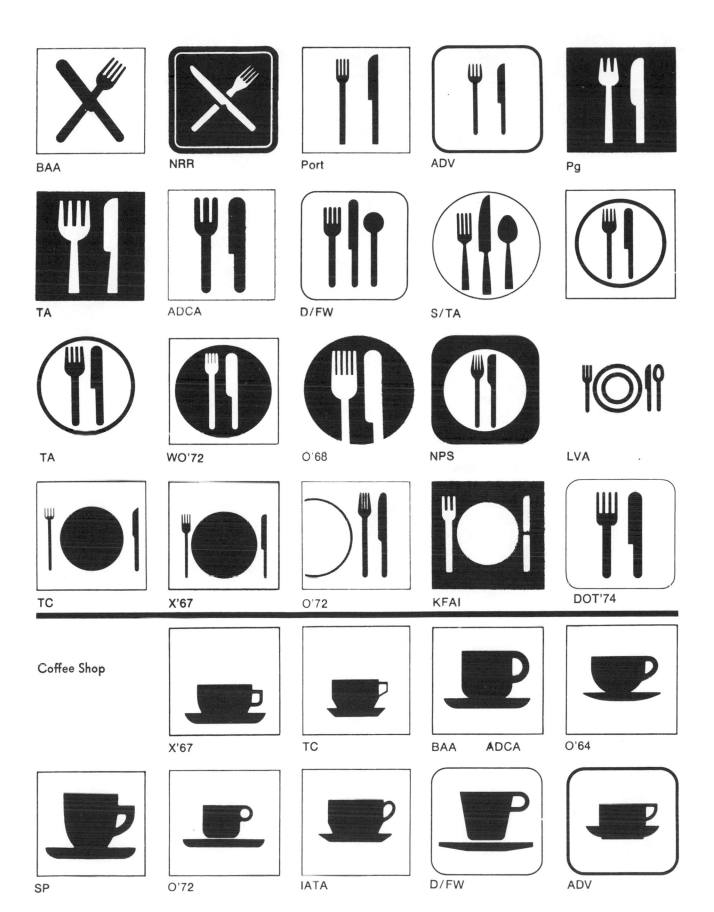

BAA

NRR

Port

ADV

Pg

TA

ADCA

D/FW

S/TA

TA

WO'72

O'68

NPS

LVA

TC

X'67

O'72

KFAI

DOT'74

Coffee Shop

X'67

TC

BAA   ADCA

O'64

SP

O'72

IATA

D/FW

ADV

ICAO

NRR

KFAI

TA

S/TA

O'68

Port

Pg

WO'72

D/FW

S/TA

DOT'74

Bar

S/TA

BAA ADCA

Port

TC

UIC

D/FW

Pg

ICAO

O'72

DOT'74

Shops

O'72

O'64

S/TA

Pg

TA

O'68

WO'72

D/FW

D/FW

S/TA

O'72

Pg

NRR

TC

DOT'74

Baggage Check-in

BAA

ADCA

Port

ICAO

UIC

O'72

NRR

TC

S/TA

ATA

D/FW

DOT'74

Ticket Purchase

ICAO

D/FW

ATA

O'64

WO'72

O'72

UIC

NRR

LVA

DOT'74

Baggage Claim

D/FW

S/TA

ATA

BAA

ICAO

D/FW

ADCA

UIC

O'72

Port

TA

ADV

Pg

LVA

TC

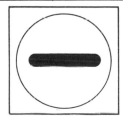
IATA

DOT'74

Customs

BAA

UIC

ADV

D/FW

Pg

O'72

TC

DOT'74

Immigration

Pg

D/FW

S/TA

ATA

O'72

TC

DOT'74

No Smoking

O'72

X'70

Port

KFAI

ICAO

ADCA

TC

Pg

BAA

D/FW

TA

S/TA

UIC

ADV

O'68

X'67

NPS

ATA

IATA

DOT'74

Smoking

X'70

KFAI

Pg

UIC

O'68

DOT'74

No Parking

NPS

D/FW

O'72

Pg

DOT'74

Parking

WO'72

S/TA

O'72

ATA   D/FW

KFAI

Pg

TA

NPS

NRR

TC

DOT'74

No Entry

TA

Pg

Port

IATA

BAA

D/FW

KFAI

S/TA

TC

ICAO

WO'72

X'70

UIC

NRR

ADV

DOT'74

Handicapped

DOT'74

ADCA, Australian Department of Civil Aviation
Telephone
Mail
Baggage lockers
Elevator

Toilets, men
Toilets, women
Information
Bus

Air transportation
Car rental
Restaurant
Coffee shop

Bar
Baggage check-in
Baggage claim
No smoking

ADV, German Airport Authority
Telephone
Mail
Currency exchange
First aid

Lost and found
Baggage lockers
Elevator
Toilets, men

Toilets, women
Toilets
Information
Bus

Air transportation
Heliport
Car rental
Restaurant

Coffee shop
Baggage claim and
      baggage storage
Customs
No smoking

Departure
Arrival
Gate
Baggage trolley

Post office, telegrams
Mail box
Stamps
Shower

Bath
Hairdresser
Nursery
Porter

Meeting point
Taxi
Railway
No entry

No dogs allowed

**ATA, Air Transport
Association**
 Telephone
 Currency exchange
 First aid
 Lost and found

Elevator
Toilets, men
Toilets, women
Information

Taxi
Bus
Car rental
Ticket purchase

Baggage check-in
Baggage claim
Customs
No smoking

Parking
Departing flights
Arriving flights
Passengers only

Waiting room
(lounge)
Nursery

BAA, British Airports Authority
Telephone
Mail
Currency exchange
First aid

   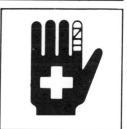

Baggage lockers
Elevator
Toilets, men
Toilets, women

Toilets
Information
Taxi
Bus

Air transportation
Car rental
Restaurant
Coffee shop

Bar
Baggage check-in
Baggage claim
Customs

No smoking
No entry

**D/FW, Dallas-
Fort Worth**
   Telephone
   Mail
   Currency exchange
   First aid

Lost and found
Baggage lockers
Elevator
Toilets, men

Toilets, women
Toilets
Information
Hotel information

Taxi
Bus
Ground
   transportation
Heliport

Car rental
Restaurant
Coffee shop
Bar

Shops
Shops (alternate
    symbol)
Ticket purchase
Baggage check-in

Baggage claim
Baggage claim
    (alternate symbol)
Immigration
Customs

No smoking
No parking
Parking
No entry

**DOT '74, Department of
Transportation, 1974**
    Telephone
    Mail
    Currency exchange
    First aid

Lost and found
Baggage lockers
Elevator
Toilets, men

Toilets, women
Toilets
Information
Hotel information

Taxi
Bus
Ground
transportation
Rail transportation

Air transportation
Heliport
Water
transportation
Car rental

Restaurant
Coffee shop
Bar
Shops

Ticket purchase
Baggage check-in and
claim
Customs
Immigration

Smoking
No smoking
Parking
No parking

No entry
Handicapped

IATA, International Air Transport Association
    Telephone
    Mail
    Currency exchange
    First aid

Lost and found
Baggage lockers
Elevator
Toilets, men

  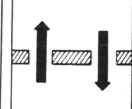 

Toilets, women
Information
Hotel information
Taxi

Bus
Rail transportation
Restaurant
Coffee shop

Baggage claim
No smoking
No entry

ICAO, International Civil Aviation Organization
  Telephone
  Mail
  Currency exchange
  First aid

Lost and found
Baggage lockers
Elevator
Toilets, men

Toilets, women
Toilets
Information (general)
Hotel information

Taxi
Bus
Rail transportation
Heliport

Car rental
Restaurant
Coffee shop
Bar

Ticket purchase
Baggage check-in
Baggage claim
No smoking

No entry
Arrivals
Departures
Left luggage

Porters
Passenger flight
  information
Passengers only
Connecting flights

Telegrams
Drinking water
Nursery
Pharmacy

Rendez-vous point
Air cargo

KFAI Sweden
  Telephone
  Mail
  Baggage lockers
  Elevator

Toilets, men
Toilets, women
Toilets
Information

Restaurant
Coffee shop
No smoking
Smoking

Parking
No entry
Handicapped
Nursery

Play room
Drinking water
Checkroom
Entry

Exit
Escalator up
Escalator down
Stairway up

Stairway down
Kennel
No dogs

LVA, Las Vegas Airport
    Toilets
    Bus
    Taxi
    Air transportation

Restaurant
Ticket purchase
Baggage claim

NPS, National Park Service
   Telephone
   Mail
   First aid
   Baggage lockers

Toilets, men
Toilets, women
Information
Hotel information

Bus
Air transportation
Restaurant
No smoking

No parking
Parking
Firearms
Smoking

Automobiles
Trucks
Tunnel
Lookout tower

Lighthouse
Falling rocks
Dam
Fish hatchery

Deer viewing area
Bear viewing area
Drinking water
Ranger station

Pedestrian crossing
Pets on leash
Environmental study
    area
Grocery store

Toilets
Mechanic
Handicapped
Bus (alternate symbol)

Gas station
Vehicle ferry
Showers
Viewing area

Sleeping shelter
Campground
Picnic shelter
Trailer sites

Trailer sanitary
    station
Campfires
Trail shelter
Picnic area

Kennel
Winter recreation
Cross-country skiing
Downhill skiing

Ski jumping
Sledding
Ice skating
Ski bobbing

Snowmobiling
Marina
Launching ramp
Motor boating

Sailboating
Row boating
Water skiing
Surfing

Scuba diving
Swimming
Diving
Fishing

Horse trail
Trail bike trail
Bicycle trail
Recreation vehicle
    trail

Hiking trail
Playground
Amphitheater
Tramway

Hunting
Stable
Interpretive trail
Interpretive auto
    road

**NRR, Netherlands
Railroad**
    Telephone
    Currency exchange
    Lost and found
    Baggage lockers

Toilets, men
Toilets, women
Toilets
Information

Taxi
Bus
Rail transportation
Rail transportation
    (alternate symbol)

Air transportation
Car rental
Restaurant
Coffee shop

Shops
Ticket purchase
Baggage check-in
Parking

No entry

    Telephone
    Mail
    First aid
    Baggage lockers

Toilets
Information
Bus
Restaurant

Coffee shop
Shops
Ticket purchase
Toilets, men

Toilets, women
Clinic
Laundry
Exit

 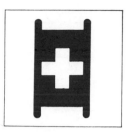  

Dressing room
Shower
Track and field
Football

Swimming
Gymnastics
Boxing
Bicycling

Shooting
Hockey
Fencing
Canoeing

Wrestling
Weightlifting
Volleyball
Rowing

Basketball
Yachting
Equestrian
Pentathlon

Water polo
Judo

O'68, Olympic Games, Mexico, 1968
   Telephone
   Mail
   Currency exchange
   First aid

Toilets, men
Toilets, women
Information
Bus

Restaurant
Coffee shop
Shops
No smoking

Smoking
Locker
Shower
Press

Track and field
Football
Swimming
Gymnastics

Boxing
Bicycling
Shooting
Hockey

Fencing
Canoeing
Wrestling
Weightlifting

Volleyball
Rowing
Basketball
Yachting

Equestrian
Pentathlon
Water polo
Wall-contact games

O'72, Olympic Games, Munich, 1972
Telephone
Mail
Currency exchange
First aid

Lost and found
Baggage lockers
Elevator
Toilets, men

Toilets, women
Information
Hotel information
Taxi

Bus
Rail transportation
Rail transportation
  (tram)
Air transportation

Heliport
Water
  transportation
Car rental
Restaurant

Coffee Shop
Bar
Shops
Shops (bookstore)

 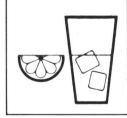  

Ticket purchase
Baggage check-in
Baggage claim
Customs

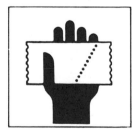   

Immigration
No smoking
No parking
Parking

Fire hydrant
Vehicle evacuation
   route
People evacuation
   route
Power source

Hole
Entrance—vehicles
Exit—vehicles
Entrance—
   pedestrians

Exit—pedestrians
Pull
Push
Detour

Stairs up
Stairs down
Escalator up
Escalator down

Freight elevator
Pedestrian bridge
Meeting place
Washroom

   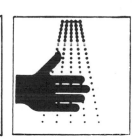

Standing toilet
Sitting toilet
Drinking water
Mail box

  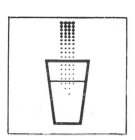 

Telegram
No entry
Toilets
No animals

Emergency telephone
Lost child office
Information (alternate
    symbol)
Television

Interview room
Studio
Press
Radio broadcasting

Teletype
Typing room
Olympic athletes
    village
Stadium

Gymnasium
Indoor pool
Boxing stadium
Velodrome

Volleyball stadium
Male athletes
Male athletes
    dressing room
Female athletes

*© *worldwide copyright of the Canadian Olympic Association. See
Notice on page iv.*

Female athletes
  dressing room
Training site
Interpreter
Official

Instructor
Program sale
Spectator seats
Subway ground
  station

  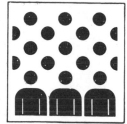 

Subway station
Garage
Car wash
Car deposit

  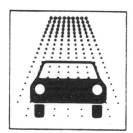 

Car repair
No traffic
Vehicular road
Gasoline stand

Take-off
Landing
Runway
Transfer point

Freight gate
Boarding gate
Send-off deck
Waiting room

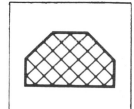   

Controllers
Duty free shop
Prayer room
Handcart porter

Porter
Baggage checking
    office
Handcart
Freight office

   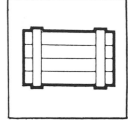

Policeman
Traffic policeman
Fire team
Buffet

Bell boy
Hotel
Front desk
Room maid

Food
Fruit
Automatic vendor
Cashier

Self-service
Stationery
Photographs
Flower shop

 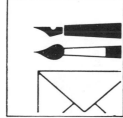  

Tobacco shop
Don't touch
Cinema
Conference room

Theater
Discotheque
Reading room
Television room

Pool
Table tennis
Dance hall
Golf

  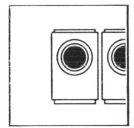 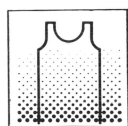

Barber
P. O. box
Dry cleaning
Sterilization

Dressing room
Tent site
Baby room
Nursery

Play room
Bath
Shower
Sauna bath

  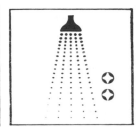 

Massage room
First aid station
Doctor
Sick ward

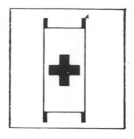   

Dentist
Drug store
Medical bath
Red Cross

Handicapped
Track and field
Football
Hockey

Boating
Canoeing
Shooting
Archery

Yachting
Equestrian
Bicycling
Modern pentathlon

Swimming
Gymnastics
Boxing
Weightlifting

       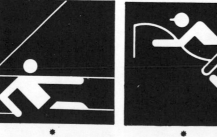       

Wrestling
Judo
Basketball
Volleyball

Handball
Fencing
Gymnastics
  (alternate symbol)
Volleyball
  (alternate symbol)

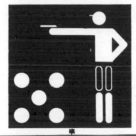   

Pentathlon
  (alternate symbol)

Pg, Picto'grafics *
  Telephone
  Mail
  Currency exchange
  First aid

†

Lost and found
Baggage lockers
Elevator
Toilets, men

Toilets, women
Information
Hotel information
Taxi

  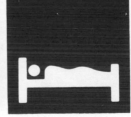 

Bus
Rail transportation
Air transportation
Water
   transportation

Car rental
Restaurant
Coffee shop
Bar

Shops (bookstore)
Shops
Baggage claim
Customs

Immigration
No smoking
Smoking
No parking

Parking
No entry
Entry
Exit

Ramp up
Ramp down
Stairs
Handicapped

*Black and red (=gray) on white field
†Red on white field

Escalator
Drinking fountain
Checkroom
Shower

Waiting room
Telegraph office
Hospital
Pharmacy

Dental care
X-ray
Physiotherapy
General medicine,
  female

General medicine,
  male
Coronary care
Hematology
Urology

Eye
Podiatry
Mental health
Ear, nose and throat

 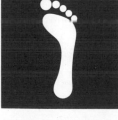  

Oxygen
Isolation
Nursery
Laboratory

Conference
Occupational therapy
Rehabilitation
Ambulatory patients

Departures
Arrivals
Subway
Monorail

Cable car
Automobile
Porter
Fuel

Motorcycle
Moving sidewalk
Ice cubes
Trailer site

Picnic area
Midway
Trailer train
Water

Swimming
Canoeing
Sailing
Marina, boating

Life preserver
Snowmobiling
Camping
Judging

Bicycling
Women's/girl's toilet
Fishing
Skiing

Soccer
Ice skating
Football
Hunting, shooting

Golf
Baseball
Tennis, badminton
Pub

Liquor store
Men's furnishings
Furniture
Cinema

Camera store
Florist
Dress shop
Shoe store

Soda fountain
Grocery store
Record shop
Toy shop

Theater
Van
Beauty salon
Barber shop

Kids welcome,
  children
Children
Men's/boy's toilet
Chest x-ray

Curling
Lacrosse
Hockey
Rowing

Reading rooms,
  library
Golf cart
Discotheque, dancing
Toboggan

TV
Travel service
Vending
Hospital (alternate
  symbol)

Danger of death
Police
Synagogue
Smoke

Warning
Seaplane
Basketwork
Church

Fire axe
Fire hydrant
Tools
Motel

Stationery store
Shoe store
Kitchen equipment
Welding

Butterfly
Vegetable produce
Deer
Elephant

Giraffe
Hippopotamus
Horse
Kangaroo

Moose
Mouse
Pelican
Penguin

Polar bear
Rabbit
Rooster
Squirrel

Seal
Air conditioning,
   winter sports
Recreation
News vendor

**Picto'grafic Safety Signs
for Factories, Industrial
Parks, Industrial
Complexes**

 *
Caution
High Voltage

 *
Caution
Overhead
Crane

 †
Danger
Explosives

 *
Caution
Men
At Work

 *
Caution
Crosswalk

 *
Caution
Wet Floor

 *
Caution
Wear
Goggles

 *
Caution
Wear
Hard Hat

 *
Caution
Wear
Earmuffs

 *
Caution
Chemical
Burn

 †
Alarm Bell

 *
Caution
Wear Gloves

 ‡
Danger
Radiation

 *
Caution
Wear
Gas Mask

108   PART TWO: PUBLIC SYMBOLS

*Black on yellow field
†White on red field
‡Purple on yellow field

 §

Eye Wash

 †

Fire Extinguisher

 †

Fire Hose

 #

No Open Flame

 §

Stretcher Station

Port, Port Authority of New York and New Jersey
  Telephone
  Mail
  Currency exchange
  First aid

Baggage lockers
Toilets, men
Toilets, women
Information

Taxi
Bus
Car rental
Restaurant

Coffee shop
Bar
Baggage check-in
Baggage claim

No smoking
No entry

---

§White on green field
†White on red field
#Black and red (=gray) on white field

SP, Swedish Standard Recreation Symbols
  Telephone
  Mail
  First aid
  Baggage locker

Toilets, men
Toilets, women
Toilets
Information

Hotel information
Bus
Rail transportation
Heliport

Water
  transportation
Restaurant
Coffee shop
Basic symbol for
  prohibition or
  obligation

General warning
  symbol
Children
Illuminated track
Illuminated
  cross-country
  ski track

Illuminated downhill
  ski slope
No entry
Dogs
Car rental

Boat rental
Bicycle rental
No dogs
No ball games

Not drinking water
Kennel
Child-care center
Scooter parking

Handicapped
Spectators
Fire fighting
First aid equipment

Protective equipment
    or device
Deep water
Shallow water
Slippery gangway

Railway crossing
Avalanche
Thin ice
Car

Boat
Bicycling
Bicycling (alternate
    symbol)
Air transportation

Pedestrians
Pedestrians (alternate
  symbol)
Pedestrians (alternate
  symbol)
Moped

Horseback riding
Rowboat
Taxi
Terrain scooter

Ski jumping
Badminton
Bandy (similar to
  field hockey)
Bobsleigh

Table tennis
Bowling
Boxing
Wrestling

Judo
Archery
Curling
Football

Athletics
Fencing
Golf
Ice hockey

Roller skis
Speed skating
Shooting
Sports area

Squash
Tennis
Weightlifting
Bathing

Ball games
Steep slope
Boat storage
Camping

Washing-up
Drinking water
Campfire
Fishing

Outdoor activities
Gymnastics
Footbridge
Guest harbor,
   boat parking

Caravan (trailer)
Canoeing
Canoe porting route
Sledding

Mini-golf
Exercise track
Tracking
Akja route

Rest area, picnic site
Own housekeeping,
   self-catering
Boat launching
Ski bobbing

Ski route
Ski track
Ski care
Skating

Tow lift
Scuba diving
Chair lift
Cabin for hire

Muscle building
Ski running,
   downhill skiing
View
Lookout tower

Ford
Youth hostel
Hiking route
Waterfall

Water skiing
Wind shelter
Cabin, overnight
Prehistoric monument

Interesting detail
Cultural monument
Nature conservation
    object
Remarkable feature

Refuse, solid
Waste, liquid
Waste, human soil
Waste, oil

Sauna
Car wash
Drinking water (tap)
Fuel

Shower
Electric outlet
Baggage locker
    (alternate symbol)
Cloakroom

Kiosk or shop
Clothes care
Playground
Change of clothing,
    women

Change of clothing,
   men
Personal hygiene
Lost and found
Outhouse

Repair shop,
   boat yard

S/TA, Seattle-Tacoma
Airport
   Telephone
   Mail
   Currency exchange
   First aid

Lost and found
Baggage locker
Elevator
Toilets, men

Toilets, women
Information
Taxi
Bus

Car rental
Restaurant
Coffee shop
Coffee shop
   (snack bar)

Bar
Shops
Shops (newsstand)
Baggage check-in

Baggage claim
Immigration
No smoking
Parking

No entry
Flower shop
Drug store
Clothing shop

Arts and crafts shop
Candy shop
Stairway
Nursery

Duty free shop
Barber shop
Beauty shop
Public stenographer

TA, Tokyo Airport
  Telephone
  Currency exchange
  Toilets, men
  Toilets, women

ARRANGED BY SYSTEM   117

Toilets
Information
Taxi
Taxi (alternate
    symbol)

Bus
Bus (alternate symbol)
Car rental
Restaurant

Restaurant (alternate
    symbol)
Coffee shop
Shops
Baggage claim

No smoking
Parking
No entry

**TC, Transport Canada,
Airports**
    Telephone
    Mail
    Currency exchange
    First aid

Lost and found
Baggage lockers
Elevator
Toilets

118   PART TWO: PUBLIC SYMBOLS

Information
Hotel information
Taxi
Bus

Car rental
Restaurant
Coffee shop
Bar

Shops (bookstore)
Baggage check-in
Baggage claim
Customs and
    immigration

No smoking
Parking
No entry
Handicapped

Checkroom
Nursery
Drug store
Barber shop

Telegram
Escalator up
Staircase up
Escalator down

Staircase down Handicapped elevator Freight elevator Tobacco shop			
Shoe shine Departures Arrivals Porter			
Hotel No dogs Push cart Send-off deck			
Gates Police Garage Shops (gift)			

2 - 6 ✈

Police

UIC, International
Union of Railways
  Telephone
  Mail
  Currency exchange
  First aid

Lost and found Baggage lockers Toilets, men Toilets, women			

Toilets Information Taxi Bus			
Rail transportation Air transportation Water transportation Car rental			
Restaurant Bar Ticket purchase Baggage check-in			
Baggage claim Customs No smoking Smoking			

No entry
Seat reservation
  office
Left luggage office
Baggage check-in
  (alternate symbol)

Porter Car sleeper train Mail, post office (alternate symbol) Telegram			

Drinking water				
Sleeper reservations				
Couchette reservations				
Sleeper and couchette reservations				

Waiting room				
Waiting room for mothers with children				
Bath				
Shower				

Hairdresser (barber)				
Chemist (drug store)				
"Europabus"				
No entry (alternate symbol)				

Exit		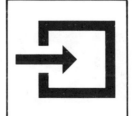		
Entrance				
Subway beneath tracks				
Bridge over tracks				

Seat for disabled persons		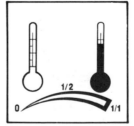		
Heating control				
Ventilation control				
Washroom				

Not drinking water				
Don't throw anything out of window				
Compartment for mothers with children				
Light switch				

Socket for electric
razor
Loudspeaker volume
Pedal-operated
facility
Do not open before
train has stopped

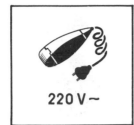   

Receptacle for used
towels
Rubbish
Car ferry

**WO'72, Winter Olympic
Games, Sapporo, 1972**
Telephone
Mail
Currency exchange
First aid

Baggage lockers
Toilets, men
Toilets, women
Information

Bus
Taxi
Restaurant
Coffee shop

Shops
Ticket purchase
Parking
No entry

Sauna
Bath
Shower
Dressing room

Baggage checkroom
 (cloakroom)
Telegrams
Entrance/Exit
Athletes

Officials
Press
Police
Interview room

Olympic village
Opening ceremony
Closing ceremony
Cross-country

Jumping
Combined cross-
 country and
 jumping
Downhill
Slalom

Giant slalom
Speed skating
Figure skating
Ice hockey

Biathlon
Bobsleigh
Luge (small Swiss
  coasting sled)

X'67, Expo 67, Montreal
Telephone
First aid
Lost and found
Baggage lockers

Toilets, men
Toilets, women
Bus
Water transportation

Restaurant
Coffee shop
No smoking and
  no flame
No entry

Entrance
Exit
Don't touch
Electricity

No standing
No sitting
No littering
Hospital

Cloakroom
Handicapped
Delivery (entrance)
Marina

X'70, Expo 70, Osaka
Telephone
Mail
Currency exchange
First aid

Lost and found
Baggage lockers
Toilets, men
Toilets, women

Information
Taxi
Bus
Rail transportation

Snack bar
No smoking
Smoking
No entry

Lost children
Don't touch
Stroller
Handicapped

Guard
Escalator
Stairway
Monorail

Baggage checkroom
  (cloakroom)
Press
Electric equipment

Grenoble Winter Olympics, 1968
 Flame
 Hockey
 Figure skating
 Speed skating

Bobsleigh
Cross-country
 skiing
Jumping
Biathlon

Downhill
Slalom
Luge

Nova Scotia Department of Tourism
 Information
 Telephone
 First aid
 Hospital

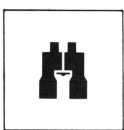   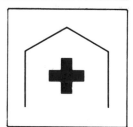

View point
Natural phenomena
Historic point
Historic church

Historic building
Church
Museum
Harbor

Snowmobile
Liquor store
Accommodation
Cabin

Motel
Hotel
Television
Color television

Coffee shop
Restaurant
Bar
Indoor recreation

   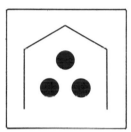

Picnic area
Picnic shelter
Drive-in cinema
Campsite

Trailer park
Trailer sanitary
    station
Individual sewage
Water

 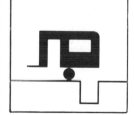 

Laundry
Shower
Electrical outlet
Men and women
    allowed

Men only
Women only
Toilets
Toilets, men

Toilets, women
Playground
Hiking trail
Downhill skiing

Horseback riding
Golf
Tennis
Hunting

Archery
Sulky racing
Freshwater fishing
Swimming beach

Swimming with
    facilities
Lighthouse
Canoeing
Saltwater fishing

Boat launch
Car ferry
Wildlife
Crafts

European Road Signs
  Right bend (left if
    reversed)
  Double bend
  Dangerous bend
  Dangerous descent

Steep ascent
Carriageway narrows
Carriageway narrows
  (alternate symbol)
Swing bridge

Road leads onto quay
  or river bank
Uneven road
Ridge
Dip

Slippery road
Loose gravel
Falling rocks
Pedestrian crossing

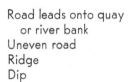
Cyclists entering or
  crossing
Cattle crossing
Deer crossing

Road works
Light signals
Airfield
Cross-wind

Two-way traffic
Danger
Intersection
Intersection with
    secondary road

Intersection with
    secondary road
Intersection with
    secondary road
Roundabout
Level-crossing with
    gates

Other level-crossings
Intersection with
    tramway
Level-crossings,
    approaches to
    "Yield" sign

Advance warning of
    "yield" sign
Stop sign, new
Stop sign, old
Priority road

End priority road
Priority, oncoming
    traffic
Priority over
    oncoming traffic
Level crossing

Level crossing
    (alternate sign)
Level crossing
    (alternate sign)
No entry
No entry, both
    directions

No entry—
    motorcycles
No entry—bicycles
No entry—mopeds
No entry—goods
    vehicles

No entry—
    pedestrians
No entry—animal-
    drawn vehicles
No entry—handcarts
No entry—power-
    driven vehicles

Maintain 70 meter
    separation
No left turn
No U-turns
No passing

Maximum speed
Horn blowing
    prohibited
Customs—stop
End of traffic
    restrictions

End of speed limit
End of no passing
Bicycle path
Footpath

Horse path
Minimum speed
End minimum speed
Snow chains required

Parking on alternate
   days
Short-term parking
Parking restricted
Standing and parking
   restricted

Parking—even dates
   only
Parking—odd dates
   only
Parking
End of restricted
   parking zone

Tourist information
First aid station
Breakdown service
Telephone

Fuel
Hotel or motel
Restaurant
Coffee shop,
   cafeteria

Picnic site
Starting point for
   walks
Camping site
Caravan (trailer)
   site

Camping and
   caravan site
Youth hostel

United States Road Signs
    Stop
    No U-turn
    No left turn
    No trucks

Keep right
Two-way traffic
Divided highway
End divided highway

Low clearance
Merge
Signal ahead
School

School crossing
Pedestrian crossing
Road slippery
    when wet
Hill

Yield
No entry
No bicycles
Bicycle crossing

   (no bicycles / bicycle crossing)

Cattle crossing
Farm machinery
    crossing
Deer crossing
Hospital

Camping
Camping (trailer
   camp)
Picnic area
Telephone

D.O.T. Hazard Labels

U. S. Weather Bureau:
Cloud Code Charts
   Cumulus humilis
   Cumulus congestus
   Cumulonimbus calvus
   Stratocumulus

Stratus
Cumulus fractus of
   bad weather
Cumulonimbus
   capillatus
Altostratus
   translucidus

Altostratus opacus
Altocumulus
   translucidus
Altocumulus
   translucidus
   undulatus
Altocumulus opacus

136   PART TWO: PUBLIC SYMBOLS

Cirrus fibratus
Cirrostratus covering
  whole sky

INDEX

All symbols are indexed except for those in Sections I and III (for which see Table of Contents):